Mayan Civilization

The True and Surprising History and Mystery of the Mayan Calendar, Ruins, Religion, and Gods

Table of Contents

Introduction:
Who were the Maya?

I want to thank you and congratulate you for downloading the book, *"Mayan Civilization: The True and Surprising History and Mystery of the Mayan Calendar, Ruins, Religion, and Gods"*.

The term "Mayan people" refers to the ancient civilization of Central America that peaked around the very first millennium, but it also refers to a modern day culture that exists across the globe. This civilization, contrary to modern depictions, wasn't ever unified, but instead was made up of multiple smaller states, where kings ruled, and each state centered around an individual city. At times, the stronger of states in the Maya culture could take over or dominate weaker ones, benefiting from the labor of the weaker state.

Features shared by Mesoamerican Cultures of the Time:

This culture had a few characteristics in common with various other cultures of Mesoamerica, like the Aztecs, Zapotec, and the Olmen peoples, but also had distinct features unique to them. For example, the Mayan people possessed the one and only system for writing that stood for the language that they actually spoke. Other cultures around that time period used writing of a pictographic nature, but the Mayan people were the only ones who had a writing system that was fully developed. Actually, a lot of features of this culture was perfected or refined in a way that other cultures did not yet have.

Although the other cultures around that time shared similar styles of architecture and art, the Maya seemed to have the best. Due to advanced networks for trading, all cultures in Mesoamerica influenced each other. In this introduction, we will briefly give an overview of some unique characteristics of their culture, which will be covered in greater detail in the chapters of this book.

Geography of the Areas Inhabited by the Maya:

The Mayan people existed in the south of Mexico, as well as the Northern area of Central America, including Belize, Honduras, El Salvador, and Guatemala. This location also includes the southern highlands, central lowlands, and northern lowlands. In these locations are savannas, rainforests, swampy areas, peaks and plateaus. Due to the rich variance in these landscapes, plenty of diverse plants and wildlife existed here, and the culture of the Maya adapted to this diversity in a creative way.

Spirituality and Religion of the Mayan People:

The religion of the Mayans was centered around time, and the natural cycles of it, celebrating the constant state of birth, to inevitable death, and then onto rebirth. The rituals used by these people paid close attention to cycles both of this earth and of the celestial bodies, which priests of the culture were skilled at deciphering and interpreting. Their civilization was heavily dependent on corn (maize), and the god of corn was, to them, of crucial significance and importance to their way of life. Religion was vital and central to their daily practices and beliefs. Some practices of the Maya would be looked at by modern people with shock, since it could get quite brutal. Did the Maya actually perform human sacrifice? We will cover this in chapter 7.

The Unique Architecture of Mayan Civilization:

Grand temples, pyramids, and great tombs were central in each city inhabited by Mayan people. In fact, a city that was once inhabited by the Maya can instantly be recognized by their unique pyramid building style; stepped blocks, surrounded by decadent palaces and gigantic plazas intended for the nobles and kings. There was one ritual of religion that was common to most cultures of this area, and this was a specific type of ball game that was known as sacred. The court for this game was structured to be nearby the temples. These ancient people also invented a structure known as a corbelled arch, allowing rooms to have an airy and light feel to them, giving their palaces and temples a pristine and unique grace.

Did the Mayan Civilization Collapse, and How?

Although many sources and rumors claim otherwise, the civilization of the Maya didn't ever vanish. Although some cities that they had previously inhabited were abandoned over 1,000 years ago, there were replacement cities that sprung up to take over. During the 16th century, the Spaniards arrived to take over the Mayans. They brought with them diseases that ended up having a harsh effect on the natives of the area. In addition to this, the Spaniards made the Mayan people switch over to Christianity, even destroying their religious texts and books. This is why there are so few left in modern day.

Regardless of this, some records did survive, known as codices. From this, we can fill in some gaps about our understanding about this lost civilization, and draw inspiration from their ways of life. We are able to deduce what daily life was like for the average commoner, as well as the type of food they ate and the animals they raised. We also know the basics about their structures of ruling, and the fact that women played important roles in their societies. All of this, and more, will be covered in this exciting guide, and you are guaranteed to learn something!

The Mayan People who Remain in our Modern Day:

Regardless of this, ancestors of the Mayans continue to exist now and can still be found across the globe. There are millions of surviving Maya across the world, including Central America where they originally existed. These people aren't one community, ethnic group, or entity. They possess and speak multiple languages, including English and Spanish in addition to their Mayan languages. But the surviving Maya are considered indigenous and are still tied to their ancient roots, along with more recent events of the past centuries.

All of these compelling facts about the endlessly fascinating Mayan people would lead one to wonder how they lived, what daily life was like for their inhabitants, along with many other curiosities. What could lead such a successful society into total destruction? In which ways were they actually far behind, although seemingly advanced at the same time? What factors of their culture already existed before the inherited it? Why on earth did people actually believe that the world was going to end in December of the year 2012? In this book you will learn about the ancient roots of this civilization, which spanned across many cities, as well as what set these people apart, and what eventually became of them.

Thanks again for downloading this book. You made a great choice, and I hope you enjoy it!

information is without contract or any type of guarantee assurance.

The trademarks that are used are without any consent, and the publication of the trademark is without permission or backing by the trademark owner. All trademarks and brands within this book are for clarifying purposes only and are the owned by the owners themselves, not affiliated with this document.

Chapter 1:
Clues to the Origins of the Mayan People

Humans existed before the Mayan people came along, but something about this civilization allowed them to enjoy advancement in a sense that other cultures had not yet dreamed of. Much of this remains shrouded in mystery, since countless artifacts of history, including books and sacred texts, were destroyed. But clues still remain. So, what can we learn about the Maya from the clues that remain? And was it about the origins of the Maya that gave them these distinct advantages over other cultures?

The Role of Efficient Farming in the Flourishing of the Mayans:

General gatherers and hunters were present in the Central area of America throughout the past millennia. Although they were common, the period known as the Pre-classic era was when the concept of permanent villages really began to flourish. This pre-classic period was responsible for truly efficient farming, which allowed villages to be inhabited densely, and this was found consistently among the area where Mayan people lived. Farming became more effective at this time because of a stronger and more productive type of corn, and a process for processing it. This method entailed soaking the corn in lime juice (or an equivalent), and then cooking it, which increased the value of the corn on a nutritional level exponentially.

The Influence of Other Societies on the Mayans:

Around this time period, the Mayan people drew heavy influence from a group of people that lived to their west. These people were called the Olmec people. The Olmec people might have been the first to devise the calendar that would become nearly synonymous with the word "Mayan". In addition to this, a discovery recently of a site used for ceremonies dates back to the year 1000 B.C. This discovery shows more about the Olmec culture, the Mayans, and their relationship, which seems to have been quite complex. There were major changes on a social scale that occurred through neighboring regions interacting with one another.

But, did the Olmec truly inspire the people of Mayan culture? Although this seems like a reasonable assumption based on evidence, it actually appears as though the whole region (including the Olmec and Maya) went through a shift at the same time, switching to styles of architecture and ceremony that were similar. This makes it seem as though the Maya weren't getting this sophisticated innovation centuries later by another culture, but that innovations shown by the Mayans might have come from somewhere known as Ceibal, or somewhere similar.

Ceibal, and what this New Discovery Points to:

The oldest known ceremonial site of the Mayans was found in the lowlands of Central America, and appears to be 200 years older than similar areas found within that region. This plaza, called Ceibal, which was only excavated recently, likely was a site for observing the sun and performing rituals, and was found along with pyramids. This finding suggests that what we thought we knew about the Maya may be wrong. The evidence points to the civilization of the Mayans being even more complicated than we initially thought and assumed. Scientists debate hotly over whether these ancient peoples, who are most famous for their calendar system, grew on their own, or were inspired largely by a previous advanced culture. This new evidence points to an answer; neither.

The Oldest Compound for Ritualistic Behaviors:

Scientists have uncovered evidence of ancient dwellings and residences in the area of Ceibal. The most ancient layers of this place were covered in meters upon meters of dirt and more recent buildings and homes. This new evidence is the result of nearly a decade of excavation work at the site of Ceibal, which exists in Guatemala and was continuously inhabited for two millennia. Reaching the very first buildings in these layers wasn't an easy task, because of hundreds of years of construction blocking the way. The structures that were discovered recently, which existed at the earliest time, have a large plaza complete with a building on the western side and a platform on the eastern side. This pattern is familiar to studiers of Maya sites, and can also be seen at the center of Olmec structures, near the Gulf coast of modern day Mexico.

A Mysterious Change that Affected the Entire Region:

Researchers who uncovered this used a dating method known as radiocarbon to figure out when it was built, and the year 1000 B.C. comes up. Since the believed date of construction is

1000 B.C., the structures at the Ceibal site appear to be a couple of centuries older than the Olmec structures near the gulf coast. This means that the construction by the Olmec could not have been Mayan-inspired. Rather, it seems as though that whole region went through a chance during this period of time, with cultures of those areas borrowing from each other's styles of ritual and building, changing them and coming up with their own unique additions.

The Olmec people had an even earlier center which had a downfall around the time 1150 B.C. However, the inhabitants at that location weren't known to have built these unique structures for ceremonial work. By the year 800 B.C. or so, the Mayan people at the Ceibal location had changing their platform to resemble a pyramid structure. This was built upon until it grew to nearly 30 feet high by the year 700.

The Beginning of a Civilization:

The phase here of the culture of the Maya people happened long before they started developing language on a written scale, and also before they used their famous calendar method. For this reason, there isn't much that can be known about the beliefs of these ancient people. However, the plaza and pyramid location had to have been used for ceremonies and rituals, logically. Within these excavation sites, multiple axes have been discovered, believed to have been placed in the area as religious offerings to gods.

Observatories in the Location of Ceibal for Solar Activity:

The layout of architecture here was called "group-E" building. These structures show up throughout the entirety of the Maya's homes and were used as observatories for solar activity. From a western perspective, one doing the viewing could see either the pyramid or the platform to the east, complete with posts on the ends and right in the middle. During summer solstices each year, the sun would rise right over the market to the north. And during the equinoxes of fall and spring, the sun would rise right in the middle, by the marker at the center. During the solstice of winter, the sunrise would occur at the very south.

The ones who first settled in the area of Ceibal already possessed an idea about the makings of villages that was quite advanced. The development of hunting-gathering ways to a lifestyle of horticulture, to living in one place and utilizing agriculture all happened extremely quickly. We can't say for sure what motivated the Maya living in the lowlands to shift from their partially settled ways to living in cities and villages permanently. One possible explanation is that the production of corn started growing in efficiency near the year 1000 B.C.

The Advantage of the Olmec over the Maya:

The people near the coast, the Olmec, had already mastered this easily, since they had the benefit of rivers full of fertile soil near the gulf. The Mayan's area of lowlands, however, weren't as wet, and were far less fertile, and had fewer fowl and fish that the Olmec people likely used to contribute to what they ate. If the farming of corn started growing in efficiency near the year 1000 B.C., this could have pushed the Mayan people to settle more permanently instead of continuing to move around so much. Around this time, it would have made much more sense to remove trees in the lowland area and start focusing on a way of living that centered on agriculture, to ensure their own survival and ability to thrive.

Ongoing Research of the Area and What it could Mean:

Researchers of this area are trying to analyze the environment and get a higher understanding of the weather and climate in that area during the settlement period. What can be assumed at this point, experts say, is that the civilization of the Maya didn't necessarily come out of a civilization that was earlier and failing, as was previously believed. The studies being done at that area are not only about the Maya specifically, but about the general way that society develops and changes with time and influence. The findings at Ceibal suggest that new cultures don't have to come out of the crumbling structure of previous cultures, but can come about via group interaction and the trading of knowledge.

There is Always more to Learn and Discover about History:

What this new research reminds us of, is the levels of hidden knowledge that still lie buried out there. There is so much more we can learn about our own story of development and evolution, including the development of the Maya. Perhaps even more research will emerge in later years that will disprove all that we thought we knew; only time will tell.

Chapter 2:
Tikal, the Capital City

In order to get to know any civilization, a look at their capital city is necessary, so what can be known about the capital city of the Mayans? The modern area of the world known as Guatemala was once known as Tikal, an ancient city of the Mayan people, which peaked from the year 600 B.C. to about 900 A.D. or so, according to estimations. Beginning modestly, with just a few structures, it later on grew to a grand city-state of the Maya, boasting over 20 different great pyramid structures. Let's look at some more of this grand place's features, which give an accurate depiction of what the Maya held dear.

Tikal, the Capital Waterhole City of the Maya:

The name of this city, Tikal, translates to the concept of being near a waterhole, and is a Mayan name. The ancient inhabitants of the city didn't call it this, however, since the name came about before the city collapsed. In modern day, this area is among the biggest sites of archaeological excavation in all of Central America. The location is surrounded by a park called the Tikal National Park. At its highest point, between the years 682 and 909 A.D., Tikal existed over the span of about 50 miles squared. The city had a population that was believed to be 100,000 citizens, with trading on an external level fueling this amazing level of growth. Research done more recently has shown that the citizens of this city had made a complex system for managing water that allowed them to thrive and survive during periods of less or no rainfall.

The Influence of a Neighboring City on Tikal:

Similar to other cities inhabited by Mayans, the people at Tikal utilized a writing system known as the glyptic method. This system used both perishable matter (from tree bark, which has long since disintegrated) and stone to write upon. Studiers of this were able to translate much of these written records and, in addition to the excavation findings, were able to learn much about the past of this great city. During much of Tikal's history, the city was under influence and possibly even the control of Teotihuacan, a close by urban area.

This area was located in Mexico, near the central part, and existed hundreds of miles away (about 600). Writing from the Mayans calls this city the reed of a cattail, using a glyph, and depictions of art from Teotihuacan show a rain god, and were found in the city of Tikal. We can assume the influence of the city of Teotihuacan due to a record from the year 379 A.D. This record states that a ruler came to ascend over Tikal, and was shown holding a spear and wearing shells and feathers (all of which are associated with Teotihuacan people).

Structures of Double Pyramids:

The incredible, and very famous, construction of pyramids was inspired, at least partially, by the calendar of the Maya people. Beginning around 672 A.D., rulers of the city would build a complex of twin pyramids at the closing of every period of 20 years. All of these structures would have a flat top, and were built adjacently with the others, containing staircases on either side of the structure. In between these pyramids existed a grand plaza, with structures built from the northern area to the southern.

An example from early on, of this structure, was created by someone named Ah Cacau, a ruler of the period. This consisted of a building built on the southern side, complete with nine doorway structures. To the northern area, there is an enclosure with an altar inside. Altogether, there have been nine double pyramid structures discovered in the capital city of Tikal. It appears as though the building of them continued on up until the city came to an end.

The Northern Acropolis Area:

During the time when the city was still new, there was an area used for the burying of elite citizens of Tikal, particularly the kings and rulers. This area exists to the north and is therefore called the "North Acropolis". This area has within it a complicated grouping of tombs, shrines, and temples. These have been built and rebuilt countless times throughout the history of Tikal. These structures cover nearly three acres of land and are rich with history about the elite of Tikal.

Special Temple Pyramids for Ancient Rulers of Tikal:

Along with these double pyramid structures, rulers from Tikal would also build pyramids to be used as temples. Six of these existed, and served to represent a ruler's burial place. There are two today which are called simply Temple I and Temple II, that are sitting facing each other. These exist in the very middle of Tikal and have a grand plaza right in the middle of them.

- **Temple I:** The first temple exists on the east side and is 145 feet tall. There is a stairway that leads over a group of layers organized into nine steps each. These steps bring visitors to a room that is enclosed at the top of the stairs and depicts images of who it was built for, a famous ruler named Jasaw Kaan K'awil. This ruler had led the forces of Tikal to defeat enemies at Calakmul, their greatest rivals. The burial room for this ruler was discovered in the interior of the pyramid structure and was full of luxurious items, such as jade, the pelts of jaguars, and even intricate artwork carved into the bones of humans.

- **Temple II:** The next pyramid, which exists beside Temple I and is referred to as Temple II, is thought to have been created for the wife of the ruler that the first temple was built for. She was from a city nearby and to the southeast. Her marriage is believed to have strengthened an alliance that was politically based. The pyramid for the wife, also known as Temple II, is 125 call and was created with three different layers of steps. At the top of this structure, there is a door way, with the carving of a woman on the wood. She is depicted in a decadent bonnet, but the image in present day is badly worn down.

Tikal's Ancient Palace Area:

When heading south from the temples described above, you will come to the palace of the city of Tikal, also referred to as Central Acropolis. Similar to the Northern Acropolis depicted earlier, this area has grown and been added to many times over the course of history. This palace area was used very early on, from at least the year 375 A.D. This palace, which was modest by comparison, had stairways on both the eastern and western areas, and benches made of stone. These benches would have been used for rulers to sit upon and go about their business, likely covered in pelts from animals to make the stone more comfortable.

Throughout history, this palace grew into a full-on complex structure, complete with at least six different courtyard areas, a reservoir for water at the southern end. This shows again, that the Mayan people were a huge fan of pyramids. Near the southern part of this complex, there is a palace of five levels which produces an effect similar to a pyramid. This is complete with a grouping of staircases that allow visitors to explore the complex. To the eastern edge of this structure, there is a stand for reviewing which was built to look over a court for the ballgame mentioned earlier in this book. This game is believed to have been played using a ball made of rubber, but the rules aren't known to us in modern day. All we can know is that the ruler, along with his family members, had the privilege of a close seat to the game.

The Complex of the Lost Mayan World:

The building of the earliest known pyramid at the capital city of Tikal started about two millennia ago, and got continually modified up until A.D., at about the fourth century. At this point, the structure was nearly 100 feet tall. Today, archaeologists refer to this magnificent complex as the "Lost World" structure. This complex can be found to the southwest of the twin temples we described a bit earlier in this chapter. A grouping of burial sites near this area show that the complex was once used to bury some of Tikal's elite citizens.

The Downfall of the Great City of Tikal:

It's impossible to know every detail about ancient Mayan civilization, but we can say that the capital city of Tikal, in addition to huge portions of Maya civilization, appears to have collapsed. This occurred around the year 900 A.D. In spite of this, a few cities, like the northern city of Chichen Itza, flourished long after Tikal ended. So, why did Tikal collapse after being so grand and decadent? This is definitely a matter that is under hot debate.

What Wiped out the City of Tikal?

Some evidence seems to point to a drought wiping out the city, since using sea-based trading routes would no longer have been possible. In addition to this, the forest appears to have diminished as the city grew in size. This could have contributed to the issue, making rainfall less prevalent, leading to a harder time with crop growth. Perhaps quite ironically, once the people of Tikal vacated the area, a jungle sprung up in its place to reclaim its land, covering the area in rich foliage.

Chapter 3:
The Mayans at their Peak and Daily Life

When were the Mayan people at their absolute highest? Experts believe that these rich cultures reached their highest peak in the centuries that existed between the year 250 A.D. and the year 900 A.D. This period is referred to, by archaeologists, as a classic period, complete with multiple cities of Mayan people, blooming across portions of Central America. These cultures appear to have reached heights in art and intellectual pursuits that dwarfed those of other countries. Only a select few areas in Europe could even come close to matching their advancements. These advancements included huge populations, a functioning and excelling economic structure, and the utilization of trade for growth. All of this denote the classic era. War was also very common at this time.

The Different Cities of the Mayan World:

As mentioned earlier in the book, there is no one specific entity or group of people that makes up the Maya. They are and were, instead, much more complex than that, and exist an existed throughout many cities. Each of these cities had unique characteristics which set them apart from each other. Here are some of the most noteworthy of those Mayan cities:

- **Tikal, the Capital of Pyramids:** The capital Tikal, which we covered in the last chapter, was the top dog in the building of pyramids. They began this early on, possibly the year 672 A.D. They showed great order in their building, sticking to pre-decided plans for structuring their complexes and pyramids.

- **Palenque, the Limestone City:** This site, another great city of the Maya, became famous because of its sculpture of limestone, along with the great burial of a king (Pakal) inside of one of their pyramid structures. When this king died, his burial included up to six other humans, offered as sacrifices, inside of a tomb full of jade. He wore a mask of jade, as well. This tomb was not discovered until the year 1952, and has been called an American discovery to rival the tomb of King Tut.

- **Copan, the Hieroglyphic Temple site:** This site existed in what is now called Honduras, and is known for having a temple with a stairway of hieroglyphs. This consists of a structure, similar to a pyramid, which was built and embellished with thousands of glyphs. These glyphs exist on a staircase made of over 60 different steps. This is significant because it is the longest inscription of the ancient Mayans that is known. It is also significant because it seems to tell a rich story of the rulers that once existed in that city.

The differences that set these great cities apart prove that although the Maya is a term that is intended to encompass a vast group of individuals, they were still greatly different from each other in skill and nature. Regardless of that, some characteristics existed across all of the different cities and were distinctly Mayan.

Daily Life for Different Social Classes of Mayan People:

Similar to the way other cultures of the Mesoamerican time period worked, the way an average citizen's life would go had a lot to do with their class on a social level. Your life typically went a lot better if you were at the top of the food chain, and you typically had to work much harder if you were near the bottom. Let's take a look at who made up these differing classes of Maya:

- **The Top Class:** The social class was split into different groups, the top group being the noble families and rulers (kings). Most of these nobles were priests, prestigious warriors, officials of the government, or scribes.

- **The Middle Class:** This class was typically made up of warriors, potters, weavers, and professional traders. The culture of the Mayan people depended heavily on crops and agriculture for both trading and food. This meant that most Mayan people farmed during the season for growing. Once this harvest season came to an end, a lot of them returned to working on the construction of the vast cities of Mayan civilization.

The Commoners of Mayan Culture:

Daily existence for a commoner who was Maya consisted of plenty of physical labor. This is not to say that they didn't live satisfied or happy lives. The families of farmers did live in a simple way, but always ate fantastically. The work they did every day gave their families food, and what was left over went to others.

- **Jobs of the Female Commoners:** The women typically worked at home, grinding maize (corn), cooking food, child-rearing, working on the gardens, and tending beehives. They also weaved cloth to create clothes to wear and to sell.

- **Jobs of Male Commoners:** Boys and men, typically, were the tenders of fields where squash, beans, and corn grew. The main crop here was, of course, corn, but in addition to this, other crops grew. Among these other crops were garlic, onions, papaya, avocados, tomatoes, chili peppers, and even sweet potatoes.

Animals for the Families of Mayan Common-folk:

Certain families at the time would keep livestock such as turkeys, dogs, and ducks. The men typically hunted wild pigs, along with deer, and went fishing in the nearby oceans, lakes, and rivers. In addition to farming, the common people may have worked as limestone transporters, porters, or even servants to the elite. However, most commoners had the occupation of farming. No animals existed to help with carrying or plowing, such as oxen or horses, meaning that it was up to the men to do these jobs. The Mayans did not use any metals, and instead relied on flint or obsidian to perform tasks that required sharp objects.

A Typical Day for the Common Family of Mayan Farmers:

A family of Mayan farmers would, on the average day, begin their work quite early. On mats made of reed, the family (including extended members) would sleep together in a house with just one room. Their breakfasts would typically be made up of a type of porridge, created with water, cornmeal, and honey or chili peppers for flavoring. The boys and men would don loincloths and the occasional cape to stay warm on colder days. Girls and women typically wore long skirts along with simple blouses. Once the family had eaten their porridge, the females would begin creating pottery or weaving, while the boys and men headed off to work in the fields nearby.

Throughout the work day, the boys and men would have meals made of dumplings full of corn, metal, and vegetables. Once their work day was over, they could head home to be with their family. Once everyone was home from work, the family members would all gather for their main course meal; dinner. This usually consisted of tortillas made of dough from cornmeal, full of meat and vegetables, and the occasional fish. Then the family members would lie down to go to sleep once the sun went down.

Free Time for the Maya Common People:

But living for the Maya wasn't just about working. About once each month or so, a festival for religious celebrations would happen at the main city, where people would dance, worship gods, and sing together. The children of Maya civilization would, of course, play with their toys, like kids everywhere do. These festivals also included decadent feasts full of amazing dishes. After eating, the citizens may have watched ball games which could either be a ritual for religious purposes, or strictly for fun and entertainment of the guests watching.

More about the Role of Mayan Women in Ancient Times:

When archaeologists studied the Maya culture in earlier times, they often believed that men were seen as superior in these societies, with women acting as their subordinates. It appeared to go along with the evidence that was found at the time, and there was no reason, yet, to question this. The belief was that the roles of ruler and king for the cities were reserved for men and that in the homes and family life, men also ruled. Studies done in more recent times haven't done much to challenge this assumption. However, newer studies confirm that females played a more central role to these societies than we previously thought.

The Female City Rulers of the Mayan Era:

As the Mayan Classical era happened, specific females would hold power in certain cities, and act as ruling forces. Typically, this meant acting as regent for a son who was not yet of age, or a ruler's widow who had passed on without leaving the appropriate heir to take over his position. Females were also serving, at the time, as priestesses of an oracular nature, throughout multiple sites that were known as sacred. In the economy of the Maya, females were also present, along with being active in agricultural areas and also textile work. It's true that the majority of Mayan females lived traditional roles, acting as homemakers, but some did hold more prestigious and powerful positions in history.

Although it was not typical for women to be deeply involved in the politics of Mayan societies, there would occasionally be situations that led to a female ruler. Females went on to gain more power in politics, during the era known as the classical times, as norms changed and got increasingly complex. Females were typically not present in hierarchical religious structures, but more recent evidence shows proof of female priestesses from the era known as Post-Classical. This occurred, based on evidence, near Yucatan.

Female Priestesses and Diviners at Pilgrimage Sites:

Among this area are caves that the Mayans considered sacred grounds for sacrificial work. These were widely used sites for pilgrimage purposes, and drew in elite members of Maya societies, along with more common folk. These places were considered holy, and goddesses often served as the inspiration for them, including the goddess of the moon and the goddess of fertility. At these places, priestesses would guide the travelers along the trails for pilgrimage. At times, the women would also serve as fortune tellers or diviners for the travelers.

The Role of Women in Mayan Economic Matters:

Females did work in roles of agriculture, such as herding and farming, but they had the role, also, of producing textiles in the economy. This was for both the trading networks and the markets on a local scale. They were dyers, weavers, and spinners, producing cloth to provide family members with clothes, and they also made elaborate pieces of art using textile work. The majority of food grown and tended to by the Maya was just locally consumed, but there were some products that got widely traded, such as vanilla beans and cacao. In a few different areas, there were females raising herds of deer, making sure that there was a high enough number of deer to keep the population fed. The work done by woman in textiles and agriculture made irreplaceable contributions to the overall economy of the Mayan people.

The General Power and Economy of the Mayan People:

It's true that food gathering and general agriculture were cornerstones in the daily lives of Mayans, but they also had a complex economy that could support a system of specialists, trade routes, and professional merchants. This civilization did not create the traditional minted form of currency, but they did use other objects for money, such as copper bells, cacao beans, and special types of bread. This proved how resourceful and innovative these societies of Mayan people were. The ruling power that kings held was almost entirely dependent on how well they could exercise control over their resources.

The Importance of Resource Control for Mayan Rulers and Kings:

Since the control and managing of resources fed so heavily into the power of kings, the rulers of Mayan times managed both the distribution and production of goods that would enhance their positions of power and prestige. In addition to this, rulers controlled other commodities that were not local, but needed by the everyday, average Mayan families, such as salt.

As time went on, Mayan rulers took over larger and larger pieces of the general economic framework. Laborers in these Mayan cities got subjected to a tax for labor on their palace building, as well as the building of their public works and temples. Rulers who enjoyed victory in wars were able to control higher numbers of laborers, using the defeated people to exact tribute. This would contribute to their strength and power, economically, even more.

Chapter 4:
Astronomy and Record-Keeping

The Mayans are perhaps most famous for their advanced knowledge and record-keeping, in addition to the calendar, of course. They had a culture that was sophisticated beyond other cultures o the time, including a complicated and impressive language of hieroglyphs. So, what are the specific features of their advanced knowledge and tools? Let's go over some of the most noteworthy examples of this.

A Complex Writing System and Folding Books:

As mentioned in an earlier chapter, the Mayan people had developed a system for writing that was complex enough to stand for the language that they spoke. This was the only existing system for writing that was that far developed in a culture of Stone Age times. Their specially made script worked with more than a thousand symbols or glyphs that stood for either a word or separate syllables. They were known to create books (known as codices) that were made from paper, made with bark from trees. These books had a distinct design, which was folding up, similar to the way an accordion folds. In addition to this, they used stone to carve their symbols into, along with bone. They also painted these complex symbols onto pottery.

What did these Mayan Texts Depict?

The texts of the Mayan people depicted divination, astronomy, and rituals of a religious nature, and provide us with a wealth of information about the Maya. In fact, these are the source of the highest historical value in this regard. As mentioned earlier in this book, many texts were burned or otherwise destroyed by the Spanish invaders, due to the content which was seen as pagan and sinful. However, there are three main codices (books) that managed to survive this plight. These codices were named Paris, Madrid, and Dresden, after the cities that now house them. The Codex of Dresden has within it very specific tables of the moon, as well as Venus, and goes into detail about how to predict eclipses of the sun.

Mayan Texts Which were Later Translated:

There are other crucially important text records that were written by educated Indians who were able to summarize and transcribe records of Mayan hieroglyphs into scripts of the Latin language. Among these translated texts are a collection of chronicles detailing prophecies, divination, and myth. There is another text which covers medical information and symbols of a religious nature. But the most famous of all translated texts was originally recorded in a Mayan language called Quiche, and was later translated to the Spanish language. A priest did this translation, and the text contained cosmological material, as well as mythological information about the Maya at modern day Guatemala.

There are strong influences present of central Mexico. In this same work, there are chronicles that detail how man was created, certain actions of divine figures, along with the people of the Quiche era, and their kings. These specific remnants of text from the era of the Mayan people were not considered authoritative or sacred on their own (like the Quran or the Bible), but instead were considered recordings of knowledge and religious rituals and beliefs.

More on the Astronomy and Writing Habits of Ancient Maya:

Keeping records was important for the Mayan people, and was needed for prophecies, astronomy, and agricultural behaviors. The keeping of this information was crucial for determining which seasons would be rainy or dry, allowing Mayans to figure out when was best to harvest and plant their crops. In addition to this, they recorded motions in the heavens (like the stars, planets, moon, and sun), allowing them to come up with calendars that were so accurate, they could be used for prophetic purposes.

Records kept on a long term basis allowed the Mayan people to accurately predict the cycles of planetary bodies, along with the phases of Venus, eclipses, and the moon. This information helped to determine the times that the planetary bodies would be at the most favorable places for activities like following through on wars, expeditions in trading, the inauguration of kings, and various ceremonies of holding. This information stood as a guide for countless important events for the Mayan people.

Looking Back at these Records in Modern day:

There was one ancient text of the Maya that even captured the specific time that an astronomer of royal stature discovered a revolutionary breakthrough about Venus moving through the sky at night. This text detailed precise measurements of the patterns that Venus made of setting and rising. These specific recordings allow historians to accurately measure when this astronomer lived, which was within a quarter of a century from the early 10th century. Within this text, it's possible to see the precise moment when that astronomer had his ground shaking realizations.

The Fascinating History of the Codex of Dresden:

This Codex is a text from the Mayan times, consisting of 39 pages, each written on double-sided. This codex has a fascinating and murky history. Somehow, this text found its way from the Peninsula of Yucatan, all the way to Germany in the 1700s. About a century later, a mathematician from Germany, who had no previous knowledge of the culture or history of the Mayan people, was looking through this codex. He found a page full of numerals, and was able to see that this table contained information about the planet Venus. This happened, even though there was no known person in that time period who was able to decipher these mysterious symbols.

Again, about a century later in the 1900s, an engineer surveyed these numbers carefully, and came upon the realization that the Mayan people were then utilizing a complex method to make up for a change in their famous calendar. This change was caused by Venus, which was having a cycle that was irregular at the time. A lot of scholars out there had believed that they could make these corrections using techniques of a numerological nature, such as making up a fictional event of Venus from the past, and then predicting movements of the future based on that calculation.

Taking a Closer Look at the Text surrounding the Table:

However, not many people had looked carefully enough at the written words around the numbers on that table. This was not the fault of onlookers, because we were not able to decipher these symbols quite yet, and wouldn't be able to until much later. During this new look at the text surrounding the table of Venus in the text, someone was able to see that the ancient Mayans were able to accurately measure Venus phases. This allowed them to time events and ceremonies more accurately. What was assumed to have been a fictional event pertaining to Venus was actually a correct measurement of the planet's shifts.

Rituals about the Shifts in Venus:

The Mayan people famously performed rituals that were elaborate and tied heavily to their calendar. It is safe to assume, based on the information in this translated text, that they were performing rituals on a large scale that were directly connected to Venus and the phases the planet underwent. This explains why the corrections were made in the table of Venus. It was because they did not wish to celebrate their rituals during the incorrect time. Small, incorrect details on their calendar don't seem important when considered on a short term scale. However, throughout centuries, this inaccurate information could have led to major mismatches in rituals that were meant to happen and when they did or did not.

The Mysterious Mayan Astronomer:

The mixture of information on this text, combined with the information on the table shows that the Maya were using highly sophisticated methods of scientific observation that points to a very specific time period. This was sometime within the 10th century. A window of about 25 years exists when this particular Mayan astronomer would have been keeping these recordings. This Mayan person, who we do not know the name of, may have been staring up into the sky at night for many years, recording observations from his observatory.

Proof of Hundreds of Years of Record Keeping:

This table matches yet another recording of an event of Venus that was discovered in another civilization of ancient Maya. This civilization was known as Copan, and existed in modern day Honduras. This text was created two centuries before the Codex of Dresden, which suggests that these ancient people were recording hundreds of years-worth of data to share with future observers. Not only is the detail of these recordings astounding, but the forethought that goes into these long spans of record-keeping is incredible and noteworthy.

Venus becomes Even More Significant to the Mayans:

The records within the codex of Dresden happen to correspond with a period of time where Venus rose to greater significance in the eyes of Mayan religions. Around the year 300 A.D., up until 1000 A.D., also known as the Classic time period, citizens of Tikal, Palenque, and Copan didn't seem to have a huge concern about the activities and shifts of Venus. However, some years later, a figure emerged in the religions of the Maya that was depicted as a serpent with feathers (a lot like Quetzalcoatl, the deity favored by Aztec religion).

Chapter 5:
The Mayan Calendar

The Maya used a system for recording time that was extremely elaborate, and is likely their most famous feature or invention. This system is not used anymore in modern day, and developed completely isolated from other calendar systems used in older times. Unfortunately, this complex calendar system ended as the civilization of the Maya fell. The majority of the lasting knowledge of the system got destroyed when the Spanish invaded and took over.

How was this System used, and What do we Know about it?

Only in very recent times, the 1990s, to be exact, have archaeologists had the ability to find evidence that helps us understand these ancient people, and their fascinating system for keeping time and dates. A method for writing, which uses symbols of a glyptic nature, was created and carved onto buildings and artifacts, which we covered in some detail in previous chapters. It was also painted onto vases and written in books (though few of these exist now, as mentioned earlier).

In addition to this, the Maya came up with a system for keeping time that had within it a method called "long count". This method was able to track the measurements of time, using differing units ranging in time, from just one day, to countless years spanning millions (though this particular unit was hardly ever actually used). Opposed to what many believe, the system didn't claim that our world would end in December of 2012, and the unit which recorded million-year spans of time was enough evidence for that. We will cover more about the 2012 myth later in this chapter.

The Vast Mathematical Knowledge of the Mayans:

These people were highly skilled at mathematics, and this knowledge is thoroughly displayed in this calendar. In addition to knowing about and referring to the idea of zero, these people firmly understood arithmetic on a modular level, working almost exclusively in 20s. But, in spite of their talent for paying attention to the sky and planetary bodies, their calendar, surprisingly, does not relate to the cycles of the moon or the seasons. The calendar is only somewhat synchronized with years in regards to the cycles of the sun. It wasn't that the Mayan people were not aware of that, but they had no need or desire to sync up their calendars with solar cycles, the way that other existing civilizations of the Old World once did.

The Three Calendar Types the Mayans Used:

There was not only one type of calendar used by the Mayans, but three separate types:

- **The Long Count Calendar:** This type was mainly used for the purposes of history, due to its ability to define dates within millennia of the future or past.

- **The Tzolkin Calendar:** This was strictly for purposes of ceremony, and consisted of 13 day periods, and 20 of these 13 day periods. This calendar would go through the closing of a cycle each time 260 days passed. We do not know why this cycle is significant, but it's possible related to Venus' orbit, which spans a period of 263 days.

- **The Haab Calendar:** This type was a civil model that worked around the concept of a 360-day year, with 20 day periods. There were 18 of these periods. Near the closing of each year, there would be five days added in an attempt to make it sync up with the cycle of the sun.

The dates of both the Tzolkin and Haab calendar didn't have the component of a year, but combining dates from both will point out a near day in a cycle of 52 years.

Misconceptions about the Long Count Calendar of the Mayans:

There was no specific departure point assigned to the calendar of the Mayan people, who appeared to have thought of time as infinite, neither beginning nor ending. Plenty of mistaken nonsense was written based on the long count method of the Mayan people. It was claimed that the calendar should eventually end at some point, along with a possible apocalypse, shift in the poles, convergence of the cosmos, or massive change in the earth. Due to the very design of the long term calendar method, which is based on cycles, this is a hastily jumped conclusion to say the least. This is what led so many people to mistakenly fear 2012.

The Cyclical Nature of the Mayan People's Beliefs:

As soon as one cycle comes to an end, it spurs on the beginning of a new cycle, and this occurs without end, according to the Mayans. For this reason, the date of December 21st, 2012, had no more significance than December of 1999! Since the Mayan calendar hasn't been used for so long, any theories on trying to decipher the "end of times" using it is only theoretical, and nothing more. The peak of the Mayan civilization has been debated hotly for years and years. The date we currently assume is based upon scientific methods such as carbon dating, but we could still have it wrong by some years. For this reason, any theories on predicting modern events using this ancient calendar must be wrong.

Misconceptions about 2012, and Why they were False:

The same can be said about the era of Christianity, which could very well be a few years off. This means that all predictions about the world ending were absurd and impossible. In addition to this, the belief that an occurrence in a millennium based on Christian time-recording methods would mark the planet's date of expiration, is made using math that has base 10, and the Mayans used 20s. This, again, proves how impossible it is to draw conclusions based on the calendar of the Mayan people. Plus, 2012 is long gone, and the earth still exists.

The entire doomsday prediction of the year 2012 was a giant misconception, at its roots and from the very start. The calendar, contrary to many self-proclaimed prophets of the end times, didn't end in 2012, and absolutely no prophecies existed that claimed the world would end on December 21st of that year. Despite this, rumors ran rampant and people got paranoid. However, the truth behind his misconception may be even more interesting. A logic-brained scientist named Carlson, who studied galaxies in the distance for a living, first got interested in this doomsday prophecy back in the '70s, when he attended a conference about the Mayan civilization.

The Incredible Grasp the Mayans had of Time:

Where Mesoamerican rainforests now exist, there was once an incredibly successful civilization. These people, as we know, were able to build incredible pyramid structures, vast temples, and bustling, complex cities. At its highest point, which was about the year 800 A.D., citizens heavily populated the area, and in the cities, there were over 2,000 individuals for every square mile. A modern day equivalent of this would be L.A. These people mastered a complex language, left behind incredible clues about their day to day lives, and excelled at astrology, as we covered earlier.

But out of all of these impressive facts about the Mayan people, perhaps the most intriguing of all was the amazing grasp they had on time. The periods of time they used to record or project far outweigh modern tools in terms of length and time span. From our current, best understanding, we can estimate that the Big Bang happened in between 13 and 14 billion years ago. Several time and date references in the ruins of the Maya go back not just millions, but billions of times further than our Big Bang date. The calendar method they used referred to as the long count, was specifically designed for these longer periods of them, and is by far the most complicated system for time keeping that has ever existed.

How the Long Count Calendar Functions:

This calendar was written with typography on a modern scale, and looks similar to the odometer reader inside your vehicle. The system is a base-20 that has been modified and has rotating numbers to stand for 20 day intervals. Since these numbers rotate, it allows this calendar to "roll" and start over. This very repetition of the numbers holds the key to the misunderstanding of 2012. So, why did the Maya fall? There is one archaeologist who has a theory, which he came to using data from NASA.

Bak'tuns- One Mayan Unit for Measuring Time:

In the theology of the Mayan people, it states that our world was made 5125 years ago. This date is what modern people would call the year 3114 B.C. When this happened, the long count calendar would have appeared as a 13, and then four zeros. On December 21st, 2012, it was exactly the same; a 13 and four zeros. From the mouths of scholars who study the Maya, there were 13 Bak'tuns which elapsed between those two dates, or 13 periods of 144,000 days each. In the theology of the Mayan people, this interval of time was highly significant, but not, as some believed telling of coming destruction. There are no tablets, ruins, or stones still standing at the ruins that foretell the world coming to an end.

No Abnormalities to Support the Doomsday Theories:

Scientists in the modern day will agree with this, and experts of NASA recently spoke to review what they found. This meeting stated that there were no comets or asteroids that were heading for the earth, that were known. There was no planet that was headed our way to wipe us out, and if there was, it would have been clearly visible in the sky. To disprove this, one only needed to walk outside and look up. The sun wasn't a threat in 2012, either. It had been flaring for countless years, far before Mayan people ever stopped to marvel at it, and never did destroy our planet. At the time, the sun was coming to its highest point in a cycle of 11 years-worth of activity, meaning that it was relatively weak in comparison with the five decades prior. Accounts of the opposite being true were completely exaggerated.

How would the Maya have Viewed our "End of the World" Craze?

So, what would the ancient people who created this incredible calendar have to say about all of this? If they could, somehow, see that December of 2012 was approaching, they would have noted that that date was highly important. Some of them thought that their deities made the world over 5000 years ago, and were coming back. One specific deity was believed, by some, to be coming back to reorder the fabric of time and space, and to refresh the universe. In other words, if the prophecy was stating anything, it was that our world would be regenerated and renewed, not wiped out, devastated, or destroyed. Humans have been predicting their own destruction since the beginning of time, and the 2012 conspiracy was just the latest crazy.

Chapter 6:
Gods and Religion

The Mayan people developed an incredibly complex culture that was far behind most others at the time, before the Spaniards arrived in the area. The religion of the Maya focused heavily on worshipping gods of nature (particularly the corn god, rain god, and sun god). The religion also consisted of a class of priestly citizens, and focused on astrology and astronomy, along with the construction of pyramid temples, discussed in an earlier chapter. Some of what the Maya partook in for religious purposes was quite violent and, in our eyes, inhumane, but we will save that for the last chapter of the book.

The Surviving Remnants of Mayan Religion in Modern Day:

As we talked about before, when the Spanish arrived in the Kingdom of the Maya, they wiped out a large portion of texts related to their religion, even going so far as to burn books. For this reason, it's hard to know exactly what it was all about, or follow along with it completely. However, there are certain aspects of the religion of the Maya that still survive these days with the Indians of Maya origin, that reside in Central America and Mexico. These people practice a mixture of Roman Catholicism and also their traditional religion. The religion of the Maya was discussed heavily as time drew closer and closer to 2012.

The Creation Myth of the Mayan World:

Mayan people had a complicated and long story of their mythical origins, which was recorded in one of their surviving religious texts. In these tales, the gods who were the forefathers of the Maya made the earth appear out of a void of water, blessing its surface with plants and animals. Making beings who were sentient was not as easy, but finally, human beings were made. Among these humans was a set of very famous twin heroes, who went off on multiple adventures, including their defeat of the underworld's lords. Their story came upon a climax where the god of corn (their father) was resurrected. This makes it clear that the entire cycle of myth here was related to the fertility of maize.

The Universe of the Mayan People:

A closely held belief of the ancient Maya was that all objects or matter in this world held differing levels or degrees of sacred quality and power. In other words, they saw everything as holy, in a sense, and not just some items. Their idea of the universe depicted the domain that the Maya inhabited (the Earth), the invisible world that the celestial gods lived in (the sky), and the invisible world of water, inhabited by the gods of the underworld.

The Mayan Deity of Creation:

There multiple deities held in high importance by the Mayan people, and each of these deities had a positive and a negative side to them. But the most important one was named Itzamnaaj (also named Itzamna in some translations). This god was the creator, and ruler of the forces in this universe that naturally oppose one another; earth and sky, night and day, death and life. This figure, as the ruler of the celestial world, was seen as the Milky Way, but was also depicted as a reptile figure with two heads, or sometimes, a serpent. He was also, at times, referred to as the god of fire.

Deities that the Maya Held Dear:

In addition to the creation deity, there are some other important figures in Maya religion to be aware of. Other important deities were:

- **The god of lightning, called K'awlil.** He was depicted as having a snout that was upturned, a snake foot, and an object protruding from his forehead. This object was usually depicted as either an axe or a tube, and was smoking.

- **The god of storms and rain, Chaak.** This deity struck the clouds to bring rain and thunder, and was called Tlaloc to the Aztec people. While some Mayan farmers believed only in the one rain god, others believed that an entire hierarchy of rain gods existed. In other legends, deities of rain strike snakes, which carry rain, using their axes.

- **The god of the sun, named K'inich Ajaw.** In the tradition of the Quiche Mayans, this god created light and the days. He was also called the sun's face, and was known for medicine and healing.

- **There was also Kukulcan** (though many different spellings and translations exist), who was depicted as a serpent with feathers, and showed up on many Mayan temples. This god later on became adopted by the

Aztecs and Toltec people, and his name changed to Quetzalcoatl.

- **In addition to these gods was Bolon Tzacab**, often shown having a nose that branches and being held in the hands of a ruler, like a scepter. This god is believed to have served as the deity of royal blood or descent.

Beliefs about Death and the Afterlife:

It's clear that caves were significant to the religion of the Mayans, since they were believed to be underworld entrances. The caves were dangerous and sacred areas where dead people were buried, and rituals for ancestors were performed. What the Mayan afterlife beliefs consisted of was a perilous journey of the deceased person's soul through a place of malevolent gods. This journey took place through the deep and dark underworld, and was symbolized by a jaguar (or night symbol, for the Mayans). Most Mayan people, even the kings, would end up in this underworld. Only people who died during childbirth, committed suicide, died in battle, or had been sacrificed could go to heaven directly.

Rituals for Death:

Rituals for death were a crucial element of the religion of the Maya, and they respected the process of death greatly. In their culture, death was something to be feared, and the deceased were meant to be deeply grieved. It was also their belief that particular deaths were more important than other deaths. They relied heavily on rituals and placed great importance on them, and were sure to pay high respects to the nature of destruction shown by their gods. This meant that they made sure to commemorate those who died using traditions, and worshiped ancestors who had been long deceased.

Burial Customs for the Deceased Maya:

Mayans who passed away were buried with corn put into their open mouths. As we know, the Mayans placed great importance on corn in their culture, and it symbolized rebirth and was meant to feed the dead on their journey of the soul to other worlds. In addition to this, they also placed a stone or jade bead in the dead's mouth, so that they would have money for their trip. Sometimes, whistles crafted to resemble animals or gods, and carved from stone, would be included in the offerings for the grave, in hopes of helping the deceased get to the other world.

The Color Red, and Graves as Entrances:

The color red, for the Mayans, was significant and symbolized rebirth and death. For this reason, they would often use cinnabar to cover the skeletal remains and graves of the dead. The dead bodies were often wrapped up in mantles of cotton just before the burials. And the sites of burial were intended to give an entrance to the realms beyond this one. Each grace would face either west or north, pointing toward the heavens of Maya, while other graves were put, as mentioned earlier in the chapter, in caves, meant to provide a door to the Mayan underworld.

The practices and rituals of death for the Mayan people shifted and changed as time went on, which we can see from archaeological evidence and artwork from the time periods. Once the late period known as the Preclassic appeared, the deceased were put into their graves holding a flexed posture.

After this, the deceased were buried in a position with their bodies extended. Even later on, the important and elite members created tombs that were vaulted, while other rulers commanded that huge complexes for burial get constructed. Later on, simply cremating the bodies became the custom practice.

What Created the Common Afterlife Idea?

It can't be said for certain whether there was a custom afterlife idea before the Spanish invaded Mayan territories. The Maya of Yucatec origin thought that multiple routes existed that you could take once you died. One tomb discovered with a pot inside of it showed the relatives of kings of Mayan times, growing up from the ground like trees, and collectively making a field of trees. There were multiple types of ancestor worship for the Mayans, including the building of idols, which contained the cremated remains of the deceased. They also brought food to the grave sites of the deceased on days of celebration, and at times, temples were constructed over an urn full of ashes.

The Rulers of Maya: Were they Semi-divine Beings?

The rulers of Mayan times were believed to exist as intermediates between citizens and holy deities, and were believed to be partially divine, as well. This was why they could communicate with the gods in ways that no ordinary citizen could. As a result, the rulers were put to rest in fancy tombs full of offerings of great value. Perhaps these were meant to be gifts for the gods, or simply gifts to the deceased rulers.

No Distinction between Religion and Science:

As opposed to other cultures, the Mayan people didn't believe that religion and science were two separate pursuits, but the same thing. So they created their complex systems for astronomy and mathematics, both of which were closely tied to religious ceremony and ritual performances. Their accomplishments in math consisted of having a concept of zero (very advanced for the time), and positional notation. And in their astronomy pursuits, they were able to calculate one cycle of the sun with great accuracy, create specific charts of positions for Venus and the moon, and could predict eclipses of the sun, as well.

More about the Mayan Beliefs of Time:

We talked about this a bit in the calendar chapter, but the Mayans had a firm and fascinating grasp of the concept of time. They wanted to chart and project what would happen in various cycles, which would let them benefit as much as possible from the earth's natural ways. Their cosmological beliefs stated that our planet has been made and destroyed five different times, in some translations. Certain days, throughout the year, were believed to be reserved for certain acts, and other days were seen as negative or unlucky.

Divination Practices of the Mayans:

They performed divination practices that involved their astronomy knowledge, along with their complex time keeping system. The work of discerning which days were lucky and which were unlucky was reserved for the priests, as well as advising kings which days were the best to start a war, harvest crops, or do planting work in the fields. These people were particularly interested in the planet Venus and its movements. The rulers of the Maya would specifically plan wars to coincide with the rise of Venus in the sky.

Unlucky Days of the Mayan Calendar:

The calendar they used, as we reviewed in an earlier chapter, was highly complex and more advanced than anything seen on earth before or since. The impressive device had a sun year that was 365 days long, and had 20 day periods, multiplied by 18, with a period of five days that was seen as very unlucky and negative. Keeping this period of time in mind, the Mayan people would take the precautions necessary to protect themselves against the bad luck they felt coming.

The Mayans, a Peaceful People?

Up until the middle of the 1990s, experts thought that the Mayan people were calm, peaceful stargazers, concerned mostly with their religious beliefs and astronomical pursuits, and above violence (unlike nearby civilizations). This was assumed due to the advanced scientific knowledge they showed, their complex culture, and the text scientists were able to translate from their time period. However, since that time, most of the hieroglyphic symbols have been translated, shaping a different vision of the Mayan people. These symbols say that the rulers of the Maya started war with nearby cities, taking their kings as captives, and even torturing them.

Chapter 7:
What was Behind their Collapse?

In order to figure out what caused the Mayans to collapse, or at least abandon their home cities, we should first look at what causes civilizations to collapse, in general. The main overlapping factor in the collapse of powerful natures, like the Roman empire, seems to be a combination of factors. Another similar feature that can be found here is rulers disregarding their resources, as well as the general welfare of citizens they are ruling over. Were these factors present in the case of the Maya?

What were Things Like Right before the Collapse?

Right before the Mayan collapse, there were some noteworthy factors that could have played a part in this. These were wars that were unproductive, extravagant construction of buildings, and exploitation of water, forests, and particularly land. Historians of Mayan culture have been able to decide on a few main contributing factors that likely caused this crumbling of the culture. This is drought, overpopulation, and general warfare.

Some people believe that the civilization of the Mayan people vanished without a trace, but this is not true. Although some cities, like Palenque, Copan, and Tikal, were deserted a little over 1000 years back, there are verifiable causes for this, such as climate change, war, deforestation, or possible drought. But it is crucial to note that the Maya were not just confined to a few areas, but many, and some cities were growing as others shrunk or became abandoned. Actually, the city of Chichen

Itza still has the biggest court for playing ball in all of the Americas.

Unsolved Mysteries, and the Survival of Modern Maya:

This court is even longer than a full length field for playing American football. The rings on the court, which it is believed that teams attempted to score through, somehow, were about 20 feet tall, twice the length of NBA baskets. The fact that we cannot understand the rules of this game makes it all the more mysterious. As we covered in earlier parts of the book, the Spanish arrived on Mayan soil and brought about significant shifts in the civilization. They brought diseases which the Maya had a hard time fighting, and burned their sacred texts, forcing Christianity upon the people. Perhaps quite surprisingly, some (millions, in fact) Mayans survive today, despite the injustices they suffered all those years ago.

Possible Reasons for the Crumbling of the Mayan Empire:

The cities of the old empire of the Mayans bloomed and flourished in the northern part of Central America and the south of Mexico for roughly six centuries, all together. It is believed that near the year 900 A.D., the civilization fell apart. There are two new research projects that look at possibilities for why the culture collapsed, which point to the Mayan people as being responsible for the crumble of their empire.

- **Drought and Deforestation:** Researchers have showed that drought was indeed responsible, largely, for the collapse of the society. However, the Mayan people seem to have made this issue even worse by chopping down the canopy of trees there, in order to harvest more crops and build larger cities. Researchers say that the drought was likely aggravated by this deforestation.

- Not to say that the cutting down of trees offers a whole explanation for the drought. However, it would explain why the area appears to have dried up around that time. Simulations of climate conditions were able to provide information on how these changes in forestation and crops would affect the climate in that area. Results from this simulation showed that cutting down as many trees as they did would explain as much as 60 percent of the drought they experienced. Switching to corn, from trees, would lessen how much water gets absorbed into the atmosphere from the soil, cutting down on the amount of rain.

- **Natural Environmental Changes:** Another research approach showed a different story, or perhaps a fuller one. This explanation suggests that the abandonment and collapse of the lowlands at the time came about from complicated interactions between the people there and their environment. As mentioned in the previous paragraph, it does seem as though cutting back the forest contributed to the drought that occurred, which appears to have peaked right as the Maya population crashed and dramatically lessened.

- But this appears to be only one piece of the puzzle. The landscape becoming reconfigured could have led to lower quality soil. There is other evidence present that the landscape wasn't in the best condition, such as a shortage of a specific type of wood used in building that disappeared. There were also species of animal, like a deer breed, that appears to have declined dramatically as the empire came to a close.

- In addition to this, economic and social relationships could have played a role in the decline of the Mayan civilization. Routes for trading had changed from transitions across land to ships in the sea. This shift might have made the cities weaker on top of the changes in their environment. In the face of challenges piling up, the elite ruling class (a tiny piece of the overall populace) could not deliver what they were supposed to, increasing conflict even more. From here, it's clear that the old economic and political structure of partially divine rulers started decaying, leading to craftsmen and peasants to leave their home cities in search of better opportunities elsewhere.

- **War:** As we went over earlier, war was an accepted part of the culture of the Maya, for many years. However, its scale and intensity increased before the crumbling of their empire, leading cities to need to build protective forts. Before this, war had been commonplace, and defeat usually just meant some important people getting kidnapped. However, as time went on, war appears to have gotten worse and progressively more destructive to everyone. The pursuit of conquering neighboring land (in hopes of improving agriculture) and taking a huge number of people for sacrifice (in hopes of appeasing gods to get back to peace) increased in importance.

- We can look at archaeological evidence that shows an increase in arrows at certain areas, showing that city life was becoming more dangerous. Military threats could have played a role as well, but evidence for this seems lacking. Not many cities of the period show evidence that any destruction occurred deliberately by foreign forces.

- **Overpopulation:** This is another possible strain that came upon the Maya and contributed to production problems in agriculture. Evidence archaeologically proves that cities in the area and surrounding settlements were populated on an even larger scale than they thought previously. Worse than this, was the droughts mentioned above. But not every Mayan city went through a drought, and it's clear that some rivers and lakes never dried out all the way. For the areas that suffered a shortage of water, the failures in crops and absence of rainfall definitely make it believable that rebellions broke out amongst the people.

- This could have been the common folk (farmers) becoming angry at the rulers, leading to people leaving the area or at least the social structure crumbling. Some historical records state events described as a "descent", which hints at a dramatic decrease in population. Still, no record exists of that big of a movement in the population, only a record of the lowlands becoming completely deserted once a collapse occurred.

Many Factors Contributed to the Desertion of the Lowlands:

The above paragraphs show that there was no one specific factor that caused the collapse of the Maya, but instead that it came about as the result of circumstances. Disorder in the social structure, war, climate issues, and overpopulation all combined in the perfect sequence to bring destruction to the order that existed in that area. None of these factors would have been enough on their own, but each happened in order in such a way that collapse was entirely inevitable, and the civilization came to an end.

Thankfully, however, this collapse of the classical Mayan people did not end the culture entirely. Although the culture did suffer terrible losses, as a result of war, deforestation, clashes with rulers, and the invasion of the Spanish, they are still here. Modern people exist now who still speak Mayan, and remnants of the religion live on today. This shows an incredibly resilient group of people who had the ability to defeat any adversity and continue onward. Because of this, people still exist to pass on the traditions of this incredible culture.

Chapter 8:
Did the Maya Perform
Human Sacrifice?

Scholars who studied the Maya in earlier days thought that they were mostly peaceful and hardly ever fought amongst their own people. These same scholars saw the achievements and scientific advancement of the ancient people and assumed that brutality couldn't go hand in hand with such knowledge and expertise. But more recent research emerged that brought this under debate, and soon revealed that the Mayans were warlike and tough people who warred with each other quite often. As mentioned previously, this nearly constant war likely contributed to their mysterious and sudden decline, and we now know for certain that they often practiced brutal rituals.

Brutal Rituals practiced by the Maya for Religious Reasons:

It's been stated before, in this book, that religion was highly important to the Mayan way of life. Among the rituals they used to celebrate their religious beliefs were dramatic performing, ball games, prayer, competitions, and dance. This all sounds innocent enough, but at the center of these religious practices, was human sacrifice. This practice was thought to have encouraged fertility, show piety of the people, and propitiate their deities. It was also believed that the gods of the Maya gained nourishment from the blood of humans, meaning the bloodletting in a ritualistic way was believed the primary mode of contact to them. The Mayans thought that neglecting these practices would lead to chaos and grave disorder in the cosmos.

The Sacrificing Process:

During very important events, the victim to be sacrificed would be held down on top of a raised structure (usually a platform) or pyramid, as a priest cut into them right below their ribs, and removed the victim's heart by hand. After this, the heart would be burned, as it was believed to nourish the watching deities. Rituals by similar cultures had practices that were a lot like this, as well. The Maya believed that sacrifice and death were linked in a spiritual way to the ideas of rebirth and creation in general. In the same book that details the creation myth of the Maya, along with the heroic twins' pursuits, a story exists where a god asks for a human sacrifice and offers fire in exchange for it.

Some hieroglyphic symbols found at an archaeological excavation site shows that the idea of beheading is linked, conceptually, to the concept of awakening or creation, according to the Mayans. These sacrifices would also mark the opening of brand new eras of time, which would often mean the start of a new cycle in the calendar. These offerings given to the gods were intended to help renew the harvest of crops, along with cycles of human life, and were seen as necessary for growth and survival. At times, children would even be included in the victims.

Bloodletting for Royal Mayans:

But it wasn't just these captive and unfortunate victims who underwent suffering for the gods' sake. Nobles of the Mayan era were, once again, thought of as partially divine creatures, and royal blood was a crucial ingredient in the rituals of the Maya, especially rituals related to agriculture. In fact, the aristocratic members of Mayan societies, who served as intermediaries between people and gods, would undergo self-torture and ritualistic bloodletting in the name of religion. The more prestigious one's position was, the higher amount of blood had to be given.

It wasn't just males, but also female nobles who had to undergo this process. This processed involved the piercing of various body parts, such as the tongue, ears, lips, or genitals, with objects like the spine of a stingray. Remnants of these spines can still be found in royal Mayan tombs. The offerings of blood would either be dripped on paper, which would then get burned, or smeared across worship idols. The smoke that rose as a result would be thought to open entrances between dimensions or worlds.

Which Occasions were Human Sacrifices Reserved for?

The religious sacrifice of humans was a practice reserved only for certain occasions, and not intended to be an ordinary or everyday occurrence. Perhaps the Mayan people believed that making this a common occurrence of daily life would take away from some of the ritual's significance, but the details of this are unclear and we can only speculate. It was, instead of being commonly done, necessary (in the opinions of the Mayan people) for sanctifying specific rituals, like a ruler becoming inaugurated, or a new heir being designated for the throne. In addition to this, human sacrifice could be used to commemorate a new ball court or temple. The victims of these practices were prisoners from warfare.

The Connection of this Practice to the Mayan Ball Game:

For Mayan people, sacrifices were often related to the game they played in the ball courts. This game, involving a ball made of rubber, was catapulted across the court, usually using the hips of the players, and often had a spiritual or symbolic meaning. Images of Mayan culture display a major connection with decapitated heads and the balls, which were, at times, even made from human skulls. The ballgames would, at times, serve as a continuation of a battle that was victorious. This would often mean, it is theorized, that warriors who were captured from enemy states or tribes would have to play the game, then get sacrificed afterward.

In the city of Chichen Itza, the unfortunate victims chosen for sacrifice were covered in blue paint. This color seems to have been in honor of Chaak, the revered and very famous Mayan deity. They would then get thrown into a nearby well. In addition to this, close to the ball court at the site of Chichen Itza, a panel displays a vivid picture of a human sacrifice happening. It is believed that this shows one of the ball players being sacrificed, from either the winning team or losing, once the game came to an end.

Disemboweling and Beheading Practices:

To the northern direction of this, the tribes of the Aztecs existed, who would became infamous for a similar heart-removal process, that involved offering up the organ (often still beating) to the gods above. As stated earlier, Mayan people also removed their victims' hearts, which is shown in visual depictions that exist at historical sites, such as Piedras Negras, but it turns out that it was much more common for them to disembowel or decapitate victims. Another method for sacrificing involved simply shoving the tied up victim down the hard stone steps of their vast temple structures.

Different Methods for Different Victims:

Which method was chosen for each victim relied on who the person was and why they were specifically being sacrificed. Different victims ended up getting differing fates, but all were equally horrible. For example, victims caught as war prisoners had the unfortunate fate of disembowelment. For human sacrifices related to the sport game, victims would likely get shoved down the steps or decapitated. Often these methods for sacrifice were combined to make another type.

How Human Sacrifice related to Politics:

Rulers and kings who became captives were considered the highest regarded human sacrifices. Sometimes, a captive would get sacrificed by getting pushed down the steps, along with the game on the ball court. It seems that no one in the Mayan culture was safe from this brutal, but at the time normal, practice. Historical knowledge of such accounts shows that no matter how advanced or sophisticated humans become, it appears that violence may be inherent in societies. Was this brutal way of viewing the world part of the reason why the Maya fell? Perhaps we'll never know.

Conclusion

Thank you again for downloading this book!

I hope this book was able to help you to learn more about the fascinating Mayan people, what made them so advanced and special, and what caused their decline. New discoveries are constantly being made that help us reshape our ideas of ancient cultures, such as the Mayan people. With new knowledge comes a new level of understanding. This book was intended to bring a newer level of understanding to those of you interested in the Mayan people.

There is much to be learned from history, even if it seems unconnected to us in our modern world. We are always connected to our pasts, no matter how much time passes. Everything we benefit from and enjoy in the present day has roots in ancient times, so learning about the people that existed then can give us many valuable insights. We can also learn from where ancient civilizations erred and went wrong, and use this knowledge to better ourselves and the world around us. It is my hope that you were intrigued and inspired by this book.

Finally, if you enjoyed this book, then I'd like to ask you for a favor, would you be kind enough to leave a review for this book on Amazon? It'd be greatly appreciated!

Click here to leave a review for this book on Amazon!

Thank you and good luck!

Made in the USA
Las Vegas, NV
13 May 2025

22063552R00036